DECORATING INDIA

A JOURNEY THROUGH THE TRADITIONS AND TRANSFORMATIONS OF HOME DESIGN

DR. JAGADEESH PILLAI

Made with ♥ on the Notion Press Platform
www.notionpress.com

|| Dedicated to all wisdom seekers around the World ||

ꕥ

Contents

Contents

PRAYER

**"Om Bhadram Karnebbhih Shrunuyaama
DevaahBhadram Pashyemaakshabhiryajatraah
SthirairangaistushtuvaamsastanoobhihVyashema
Devahitam YadaayuhSwasti Na Indro
VridhashravaahSwasti Nah Pooshaa
VishwavedaahSwasti Nastaarkshyo ArishtanemihSwasti
No Brihaspatir DadhaatuOm Shantih, Shantih, Shantih"**

The literal meaning of this mantra is: OM. O Gods! Let us hear auspicious words from our ears. O reverent Gods! Let us behold propitious visions from our eyes, let our organs and body be stable, healthy, and strong. Let us do that which is pleasing to the gods in the life span allotted to us. May Indra, inscribed in the scriptures, bring us fortune! May Pushan, the knower of the world, grant us prosperity! May Trakshya, who vanquishes enemies, bestow us with blessings! May Brihaspati bring us success!
OM Peace, Peace, Peace.

ABOUT THE AUTHOR

Dr. Jagadeesh Pillai is a renowned Guinness World Record holder, writer, and researcher hailing from Varanasi, also known as the abode of Lord Shiva. With a Ph.D. in Vedic Science and a range of creative ideas and achievements, he is a true polymath. He is the author of more than 100 books including Research Publications. Although his roots can be traced back to Kerala, the people of Varanasi hold him in high regard and affectionately consider him one of their own.

In 1998, Dr. Pillai was offered a job at Banaras Hindu University, but he left the position after only two months to pursue greater goals in life. He believed that in order to study Indian scriptures and engage in other creative endeavours, he needed to retire from the daily grind of working solely for money at a young age.

He started an export business from scratch, using the knowledge he had gained from a previous job in the industry. His intelligence and unique approach to business led to great success in a short period of time, earning him more in just a decade and a half than he would have in a lifetime working in a government job. Upon the passing of Dr. APJ Abdul Kalam, Dr. Pillai decided to leave the business and dedicate himself to reading, studying, researching, and experimenting.

During his tenure in the export business, Dr. Pillai traveled to over 16 countries, gaining valuable insight and experiencing the world and life in detail.

Dr. Pillai has achieved four Guinness World Records in the following subjects:

"Script to Screen" - In this record, Dr. Pillai produced and directed an animation film within the shortest time possible, breaking the previous record set by Canadians. He has also received numerous national and international awards and recognitions for this achievement.

Longest Line of Postcards - For this record, Dr. Pillai created a line of 16,300 postcards on the occasion of the 163rd anniversary of Indian Postal Day. The event also included a questionnaire about the Indian flag.

Largest Poster Awareness Campaign - Dr. Pillai designed an awareness campaign on the subject of "Beti Bachao - Beti Padhao" (Save the Girl Child - Educate the Girl Child) to achieve this record.

Largest Envelope - In tribute to the Indian Prime Minister's "Make in India" initiative, Dr. Pillai created a 4000 square meter envelope using waste paper to achieve this record.

Attempted - **70000 Candles on a 210 kg Cake** - To celebrate the 70th Indian Independence Day, Dr. Pillai attempted to light 70,000 candles on a 210 kg cake, which was recorded in World Records India.

Attempted - **Documentary on Dhamek Stupa of Sarnath in 17 Languages** - Dr. Pillai attempted to create a documentary on the Dhamek Stupa of Sarnath, dubbing it in 17 different languages. The result of this attempt is currently awaiting confirmation from the Guinness World Records.

Dr. Pillai is skilled in teaching the Bhagavad Gita, a Hindu scripture, and is popular among young people. He has helped many young people improve their lives through his motivational teachings.

In addition to teaching, he has composed and sung numerous Sanskrit Bhajans and patriotic songs.

He has also written and directed several short films and documentaries for awareness campaigns, and has volunteered with the police in both UP and Kerala to spread awareness about various issues through videos and photography.

Incredibly, he has produced and directed over 100 documentaries about the city of Varanasi, all on his own.

He has also helped and guided more than 25 boys and girls to achieve world records through creative and innovative methods. He is a multifaceted person who uses his intellect and the blessings given to him by God to excel in various areas. He is both a teacher and a student, always learning and teaching, and is able to master any subject he comes across.

He is a selfless social activist and motivational speaker who has overcome struggles and failures to become a successful and enthusiastic individual with a rich life experience.

In addition to his work with the Bhagavad Gita, he is also an efficient Tarot card reader, Astro-Vastu consultant, and a talented singer and composer. He has sung the entire Ram Charita Manas and Bhagavad Gita in his own compositions, and has sung the phrase "Lokah Samastha Sukhino Bhavantu" in 50 different languages. He is currently working on a detailed and scientific study of Vedas, Upanishads, Puranas, and the Bhagavad Gita. He has also composed and sung the Hanuman Chalisa and Gayatri Mantra in 108 and 1008 different compositions, respectively.

Awards - Four Times Guinness World Records, Winner of Mahatma Gandhi Vishwa Shanti Puraskar, Mahatma Gandhi Global Peace Ambassador, Kashi Ratna Award, Dr. APJ Abdul Kalam Motivational Person of the Year 2017, Mother Teresa Award, Indira Gandhi Priyadarshini Award, Bharat Vikas Ratna Award, Udyog Ratna Award, Vigyan Prasar Award, Poorvanchal Ratn Samman.

PREFACE

Home decor is a reflection of one's culture, lifestyle, and values. For centuries, Indians have decorated their homes with traditional elements that reflect their heritage and values. My goal for this book, The Indian Home Decor: An Insight into the Significance and Evolution of Indian Home Decor, is to explore the history and significance of Indian home decor and the many ways in which it has shaped Indian culture and society.

This book is intended to serve as an introduction to the rich history and culture of Indian home decor for readers who are new to the subject. It explores the evolution of Indian home decor from its traditional roots to its modern-day forms. The book covers various topics, including the development of different styles and trends, the emergence of popular home decor designers, and the impact of Bollywood on Indian home decor. It also examines the economics of the Indian home decor industry and explores how technological and societal changes have shaped its evolution.

The book draws on research from a variety of sources, including interviews with key figures in the Indian home decor industry, archival materials, and cultural analysis. I have also conducted extensive field research in India, including attending home decor shows, interviewing home decor designers, and visiting locations associated with the production of Indian home decor. Through this research, I hope to provide readers with a comprehensive understanding of the Indian home decor industry and its various components.

I am deeply passionate about the art of Indian home decor and hope that this book will help to spread the appreciation of this wonderful art form. I believe that Indian home decor has a great deal to offer to the world and I am excited to share its cultural and historical significance with my readers.

A Traditional Indian Home Interior

I

Introduction to Indian Home Decor

The Indian subcontinent is a rich tapestry of cultures, traditions, and beliefs, each with its unique way of decorating homes. From the intricate carvings of Rajasthan to the lush greenery of Kerala, Indian home décor reflects the diverse customs, values, and aesthetics of its people.

For centuries, Indian families have created warm and inviting spaces that reflect their individual tastes and personalities. From the richly decorated palaces of royalty to the simple homes of farmers, Indian homes have always been at the forefront of showcasing the country's cultural heritage.

In this chapter, we will delve into the rich history of Indian home décor and explore its evolution over the years. We will look at the various influences that have shaped the way homes are decorated in different parts of the country and examine the significance of certain design elements and materials.

The History of Indian Home Décor

The history of Indian home décor can be traced back to the Indus Valley Civilization (3300–1300 BCE), where homes were decorated with intricate carvings, frescoes, and sculptures. The early settlers of the region believed that their homes were a reflection of their status and wealth, and they decorated them with the finest materials and craftsmanship.

Over the centuries, various civilizations and cultures have left their mark on Indian home décor. From the Mughal Empire (1526–1857), which brought a fusion of Persian, Turkish, and Indian styles, to the British Raj (1858–1947), which introduced Victorian and colonial design elements, each era has contributed to the rich diversity of Indian home décor.

The Significance of Color in Indian Home Décor

Color plays a significant role in Indian home décor, with each hue having its own symbolic meaning. In Hinduism, for example, red symbolizes purity, while green symbolizes peace. In many parts of India, blue is associated with the Hindu god Krishna and is often used in homes as a lucky color.

In addition to cultural and religious significance, color is also used to create mood and atmosphere in Indian homes. Bright colors are often used to add warmth and vibrancy to spaces, while more muted tones are used to create a calming and relaxing atmosphere.

The Use of Textiles in Indian Home Décor

Textiles have always been an important part of Indian home décor, with each region having its own unique styles and techniques. From the intricate embroidery of Lucknow to the vibrant block prints of Rajasthan, textiles have been used to add color, texture, and pattern to Indian homes for centuries.

In addition to their aesthetic value, textiles also serve practical purposes in Indian homes. From bedspreads and curtains to table runners and cushion covers, textiles play an important role in creating a comfortable and welcoming atmosphere.

The Importance of Natural Materials in Indian Home Décor

Natural materials such as wood, stone, and clay have been used in Indian home décor for centuries, reflecting the country's rich cultural heritage and close connection to the natural world. From the elaborate wooden carvings of Rajasthan to the clay pottery of rural India, natural materials play a key role in creating warm and inviting spaces.

In recent years, there has been a resurgence of interest in traditional Indian craftsmanship, with many families opting to incorporate natural materials into their homes as a way of preserving their cultural heritage.

The rich history and cultural diversity of India have contributed to the country's unique and vibrant style of home décor. From the use of color and textiles to the incorporation of natural materials, each element plays a crucial role in creating warm and inviting spaces that reflect the values and beliefs of Indian families. Whether it is the intricate carvings of Rajasthan or the lush greenery of Kerala, Indian home décor is a testament to the country's rich cultural heritage and its evolution over the centuries.

As we embark on this journey through the traditions and transformations of Indian home décor, we invite you to discover the fascinating stories behind the design elements and techniques that make Indian homes so unique and special. Join us as we explore the cultural, historical, and aesthetic influences that have shaped the way homes are decorated in India, and discover the timeless beauty and significance of Indian home décor.

"Home is where the heart is, and in India, it is where our rich culture and heritage are reflected in every nook and corner."

ﷺ

II

History of Indian Home Decor

The history of Indian home decor can be traced back to the Indus Valley Civilization (3300–1300 BCE), where homes were decorated with intricate carvings, frescoes, and sculptures. The early settlers of the region believed that their homes were a reflection of their status and wealth, and they decorated them with the finest materials and craftsmanship.

Over the centuries, various civilizations and cultures have left their mark on Indian home decor, shaping its evolution and diversity. From the Mughal Empire (1526–1857), which brought a fusion of Persian, Turkish, and Indian styles, to the British Raj (1858–1947), which introduced Victorian and colonial design elements, each era has contributed to the rich tapestry of Indian home decor.

The Mughal Era (1526-1857)

The Mughal Empire, which ruled over India for several centuries, had a profound impact on Indian home decor. The Mughals brought with them a fusion of Persian, Turkish, and Indian styles, which were reflected in the lavish palaces and homes they built.

One of the most notable features of Mughal-style home decor was the use of intricate carvings, frescoes, and paintings. The walls and ceilings of homes were adorned with elaborate designs, featuring motifs of flowers, birds, and animals. The Mughals also introduced the use of arches and domes in home decor, which became a hallmark of the style.

The British Raj (1858-1947)

The British rule over India lasted for almost 90 years, and during this time, they introduced their own style of home decor, which blended Victorian and colonial elements with traditional Indian design.

Homes built during the British Raj were often grand and spacious, featuring high ceilings, large windows, and ornate moldings. The use of furnishings such as sofas, chairs, and wardrobes became popular during this era, as did the use of rugs and carpets.

The Indian Independence Movement (1947-Present)

The Indian independence movement marked a new era in the history of Indian home decor, as the country began to embrace its own cultural heritage and traditions. The use of traditional materials and techniques, such as hand-woven textiles and intricate carvings, became popular once again.

In recent years, there has been a resurgence of interest in traditional Indian craftsmanship, with many families opting to incorporate natural materials and traditional design elements into their homes as a way of preserving their cultural heritage.

The rich history of Indian home decor is a testament to the country's cultural heritage and diversity. From the intricate carvings of the Mughal era to the grand homes of the British Raj, each era has contributed to the evolution of Indian home decor. Today, Indian families are embracing their cultural heritage, incorporating traditional materials and techniques into their homes as a way of preserving their history and preserving their unique style.

"From palaces to mud huts, Indian home decor showcases the diversity and richness of our country's traditions."

ꝏ

III

Traditional Indian Home Decor Elements

India is renowned for its rich cultural heritage, and this is reflected in the traditional elements used in Indian home decor. From intricate carvings and hand-woven textiles to vibrant color palettes and the use of natural materials, each element plays a crucial role in creating warm and inviting spaces that reflect the values and beliefs of Indian families. In this chapter, we will explore some of the most iconic and timeless elements of traditional Indian home decor.

Carvings and Sculptures

Carvings and sculptures are an integral part of Indian home decor, and can be found in homes across the country. From the intricate wooden carvings of Rajasthan to the stone sculptures of Tamil Nadu, each region has its own unique style and tradition. Carvings and sculptures often feature religious or cultural motifs, such as gods, goddesses, and animals, and they are used to adorn walls, furniture, and architectural elements such as doorways and windows.

Hand-Woven Textiles

Hand-woven textiles have been a part of Indian home decor for centuries, and they continue to play a significant role in the design of Indian homes today. From the vibrant silk saris of Banaras to the hand-loomed cotton bedspreads of Keralan, each region has its own unique style and tradition. Textiles are used to add color and texture to spaces, and they are often used to create curtains, cushions, and upholstery.

Vibrant Color Palettes

Indian home decor is renowned for its use of vibrant colors, which are often inspired by nature. From the warm hues of saffron and turmeric to the cool blues and greens of the ocean, each color has its own significance and meaning. Color is used to create an ambiance and evoke a mood, and it is often used to highlight specific elements of a room, such as walls, furniture, or textiles.

Natural Materials

The use of natural materials is a key element of traditional Indian home decor, and it is a reflection of the country's close connection to the earth. From the intricate carvings of sandalwood and teak to the warm glow of hand-woven baskets and jute rugs, each material has its own unique qualities and beauty. Natural materials are used to create a warm and inviting atmosphere, and they are often combined with other elements, such as textiles and color, to create a cohesive and harmonious space.

Paintings and Wall Art

Paintings and wall art play a significant role in Indian home decor, and they are used to add color, texture, and cultural significance to spaces. From the intricate miniatures of Rajasthan to the lush landscapes of Kerala, each region has its own unique style and tradition. Paintings and wall art are used to adorn walls, ceilings, and other architectural elements, and they often feature religious, cultural, or historical motifs.

The traditional elements of Indian home decor are a reflection of the country's rich cultural heritage and its close connection to the earth. From intricate carvings and hand-woven textiles to vibrant color palettes and the use of natural materials, each element plays a crucial role in creating warm and inviting spaces that reflect the values and beliefs of Indian families. Whether it is the elaborate carvings of Rajasthan or the lush greenery of Kerala, Indian home decor is a testament to the timeless beauty and significance of Indian cultural heritage.

"The evolution of Indian home decor reflects the changing times, yet it holds on to its roots, keeping the traditional elements intact."

ĸ

IV

Evolving Styles and Trends in Indian Home Decor

As with any culture, the styles and trends in Indian home decor have evolved over time, reflecting changes in society, technology, and globalization. In this chapter, we will explore the various styles and trends that have shaped Indian home decor over the centuries, from the classic elegance of the Mughal era to the contemporary fusion of traditional and modern elements that is so prevalent today.

Mughal Era (1526-1857)

The Mughal era marked a significant turning point in Indian home decor, as the influence of Persian and Central Asian styles began to take hold. Characterized by intricate carvings, luxurious textiles, and rich colors, Mughal-style homes were designed to reflect the wealth and power of the ruling class. Furniture was often made from sandalwood and teak, and it was adorned with intricate carvings, gold leaf, and precious gems. The use of vibrant colors, such as red, green, and gold, was also a hallmark of this era, and it was used to create a warm and inviting atmosphere.

British Colonial Era (1857-1947)

The British colonial era had a profound impact on Indian home decor, as Victorian and Georgian styles were introduced to the country. Characterized by elegant furnishings, crisp linens, and neutral colors, British-style homes were designed to reflect the sophistication and elegance of the colonial ruling class. Furniture was often made from mahogany and teak, and it was adorned with intricate carvings and gold leaf. The use of neutral colors, such as beige, cream, and white, was also a hallmark of this era, and it was used to create a calm and serene atmosphere.

Post-Independence Era (1947-Present)

In the decades following India's independence, the country's home decor began to reflect the influence of globalization and modern technology. The use of new materials, such as plastic, steel, and glass, was combined with traditional elements, such as hand-woven textiles and intricate carvings, to create a unique fusion of traditional and modern styles. Homes also began to reflect the changing values and beliefs of Indian society, as more families sought to create spaces that reflected their own personal tastes and lifestyles.

Contemporary Trends

Today, Indian home decor is a rich and diverse blend of traditional and contemporary styles, reflecting the country's vibrant cultural heritage and its close connection to the global community. From the use of sleek, modern furniture and technology to the incorporation of traditional elements, such as hand-woven textiles and intricate carvings, homes today are designed to reflect the unique tastes and lifestyles of their owners. Some of the most popular contemporary trends in Indian home decor include:

Minimalism:

nspired by the simplicity and elegance of Japanese design, minimalist homes feature clean lines, neutral colors, and an emphasis on function over form.

Fusion:

As more and more families embrace the fusion of traditional and contemporary styles, homes today are often designed to reflect the unique blend of cultures and traditions that make up India.

Eco-Friendly:

As more and more families seek to create homes that are both beautiful and sustainable, eco-friendly homes are becoming increasingly popular in India. This trend is characterized by the use of natural materials, such as bamboo and jute, and the incorporation of eco-friendly technologies, such as solar power and rainwater harvesting.

Technology:

With the rise of smart homes and home automation, technology is increasingly playing a role in Indian home decor. From the use of LED lighting and home automation systems to the integration of smart appliances, homes are becoming increasingly connected and user-friendly, making life easier and more comfortable for families.

The styles and trends in Indian home decor are a reflection of the country's rich cultural heritage, its connection to the global community, and its evolving values and beliefs. Whether it's the classic elegance of the Mughal era, the sophistication of the British colonial era, or the fusion of traditional and modern styles that is so prevalent today, Indian home decor is a testament to the creativity, ingenuity, and diversity of India's people. As the country continues to evolve and grow, it will be fascinating to see how the styles and trends in home decor continue to reflect the unique character and spirit of this remarkable country.

"In India, decorating your home is not just about aesthetics, it is about imbibing positive energy, good luck, and prosperity."

ꕥ

V

Diversity of Indian Home Decor

India is a land of incredible diversity, with a rich and varied cultural heritage that extends back thousands of years. This diversity is reflected in every aspect of life in the country, including the way that homes are decorated and designed. In this chapter, we will explore the incredible variety of styles and approaches to home decor that are found across India, and how these reflect the different regions, communities, and cultural traditions of the country.

One of the most important factors that contributes to the diversity of Indian home decor is the country's geography. With its vast size and varied topography, India is home to a wide range of different climate zones, each of which has its own unique set of environmental challenges and opportunities. For example, in the dry and arid regions of the west and south, homes are often designed to maximize natural ventilation and cooling, with large windows, high ceilings, and courtyards that provide relief from the heat. In contrast, in the lush, tropical regions of the east and north, homes are often built to protect residents from the intense heat and rainfall, with sturdy walls, deep overhangs, and large verandahs that provide shade and shelter.

Another important factor that contributes to the diversity of Indian home decor is the country's cultural heritage. India is home to many different religious, ethnic, and linguistic groups, each of which has its own unique traditions and cultural practices. These traditions are reflected in the way that homes are designed and decorated, with different regions and communities adopting their own unique styles and approaches. For example, in the region of Rajasthan, homes are often decorated with intricate carvings and brightly-colored frescoes, reflecting the region's rich history and artistic traditions. In the southern state of Tamil Nadu, homes are often built in a distinctive style that incorporates elaborate wood carvings, intricate sculptures, and painted ceilings, reflecting the region's rich cultural heritage.

Another factor that contributes to the diversity of Indian home decor is the country's history and its relationship with the rest of the world. India has been shaped by centuries of migration and trade, and has been influenced by the many different cultures and civilizations that have passed through its borders over the centuries. This is reflected in the way that homes are designed and decorated, with different regions and communities adopting styles and approaches that reflect the influence of the different cultures that have passed through the area. For example, in the former British colonial territories of India, homes are often designed in a distinctive style that incorporates elements of British colonial architecture, such as large windows, high ceilings, and grand entrance halls.

The diversity of Indian home decor is a testament to the incredible variety and richness of the country's cultural heritage, its geography, and its relationship with the rest of the world. Whether it's the intricate carvings of Rajasthan, the elegant simplicity of southern Tamil Nadu, or the fusion of styles that is so prevalent in modern India, each region and community has its own unique approach to home decor that reflects its history, culture, and traditions. In the pages that follow, we will explore these diverse styles and approaches in greater detail, and gain a deeper appreciation for the incredible richness and variety of Indian home decor.

"The use of vibrant colors, intricate patterns, and sacred symbols in Indian home decor is a testament to our rich cultural heritage."

☙

VI

Traditional Indian Furniture and Accessories

Furniture and accessories play a central role in the design and decoration of Indian homes. From intricately carved wooden chairs to colorful handwoven textiles, these elements help to create the unique atmosphere and ambiance of each individual home. In this chapter, we will explore the traditional Indian furniture and accessories that are used in homes across the country, and learn how they have evolved over time to reflect the changing needs and tastes of the Indian people.

One of the most important and enduring traditions in Indian furniture design is the use of wood. For centuries, Indian artisans have been using wood to create beautiful and functional furniture pieces, such as chairs, tables, and cabinets. These pieces are often carved with intricate designs that reflect the local cultural and religious traditions, and are finished with natural oils and waxes to bring out the beauty of the wood grain. In addition to its aesthetic appeal, wood is also a practical material for furniture, as it is strong, durable, and easily renewable.

Another important tradition in Indian furniture design is the use of textiles. From the soft and luxurious drapes that adorn windows, to the bright and colorful cushions that add comfort to seating areas, textiles are an essential part of Indian home decor. Many of these textiles are handwoven using traditional techniques, and feature intricate patterns and designs that reflect the cultural heritage of the weaver. Some of the most famous and sought-after textiles in India include the vibrant silk saris of Varanasi, the intricate tie-dye fabrics of Rajasthan, and the delicate hand-embroidered shawls of Kashmir.

In addition to furniture and textiles, there are also many other traditional Indian accessories that are used to decorate homes. These can include everything from paintings and sculptures, to mirrors, lamps, and vases. Many of these accessories are also crafted by hand, using techniques that have been passed down from generation to generation, and feature intricate designs and patterns that reflect the cultural heritage of the region. For example, in the region of Madhya Pradesh, craftsmen are famous for their intricate metalwork, which includes everything from fine jewelry to intricate lamps and lanterns.

One of the key trends in traditional Indian furniture and accessories is the increasing popularity of eco-friendly and sustainable materials. As awareness of the impact of consumer products on the environment has grown, many Indian designers are turning to natural and sustainable materials, such as bamboo, jute, and cotton, to create beautiful and functional furniture and accessories. This movement has not only helped to reduce the environmental impact of consumer products, but has also led to the creation of new and innovative designs that are both beautiful and sustainable.

Traditional Indian furniture and accessories play a crucial role in the design and decoration of homes across the country. Whether it's the intricate carvings of wooden furniture, the bright and colorful textiles, or the delicate and intricate accessories, these elements help to create the unique atmosphere and ambiance of each home, and reflect the rich cultural heritage of the region. In the pages that follow, we will explore these traditional elements in greater detail, and gain a deeper appreciation for the rich and varied traditions of Indian home decor.

"The art of Indian home decor is a fusion of tradition and modernity, where innovation meets the timeless beauty of our past."

ꟾ

VII

Modern Indian Home Decor Designers

While traditional Indian home decor remains popular and influential, there is also a thriving community of modern designers who are pushing the boundaries of Indian home design and introducing new and innovative ideas. In this chapter, we will explore the work of some of the most talented and influential modern Indian home decor designers, and learn how they are taking inspiration from the rich traditions of Indian home decor, while also incorporating new and contemporary elements.

One of the leading names in modern Indian home decor is Sussanne Khan, who has been praised for her innovative and stylish designs. Sussanne's work is characterized by a subtle fusion of traditional Indian elements and contemporary design techniques, and she is known for her use of natural materials, such as wood, stone, and textiles. Her designs are inspired by the beauty and complexity of Indian architecture and textiles, and she is dedicated to creating beautiful and functional spaces that reflect the unique style and personality of each client.

Another leading name in modern Indian home decor is Raseel Gujral, who has been at the forefront of the Indian home decor scene for over a decade. Raseel's work is characterized by her bold use of color and pattern, and she is known for her innovative use of traditional Indian materials and techniques. Her designs are often inspired by her travels to different regions of India, and she is dedicated to creating spaces that are not only beautiful, but also functional and comfortable.

In addition to these well-known designers, there is also a growing community of young and talented designers who are making their mark on the Indian home decor scene. These designers are often trained in India and abroad, and are bringing a fresh perspective and new ideas to the traditional Indian home decor. They are exploring new materials and techniques, and are often influenced by contemporary design trends from around the world.

One trend that is emerging in modern Indian home decor is the use of eco-friendly and sustainable materials. As awareness of the impact of consumer products on the environment has grown, many Indian designers are turning to natural and sustainable materials, such as bamboo, jute, and cotton, to create beautiful and functional home decor. This movement has not only helped to reduce the environmental impact of consumer products, but has also led to the creation of new and innovative designs that are both beautiful and sustainable.

Modern Indian home decor designers are playing a crucial role in shaping the future of Indian home decor. By taking inspiration from the rich traditions of Indian home decor, while also incorporating new and contemporary elements, these designers are creating spaces that are both beautiful and functional. Whether it's through their use of innovative materials and techniques, or their exploration of new and emerging trends, modern Indian home decor designers are helping to bring Indian home decor into the 21st century, and ensuring that it continues to evolve and grow.

"Indian furniture and accessories are not just functional, they are works of art, crafted with love, and steeped in history."

ꕥ

VIII

The Economics of Indian Home Decor

The home decor industry in India is a thriving and rapidly growing sector, with millions of consumers seeking to decorate and furnish their homes with the latest styles and trends. In this chapter, we will examine the economics of the Indian home decor industry, including the factors that influence the demand for home decor products, the supply chain and distribution channels, and the role of the government in regulating the industry.

One of the key factors that drives demand for home decor products in India is the growing middle class, which is increasingly looking to improve the quality of their homes. This is due in part to the rapid economic growth and urbanization in India, which has led to the creation of a large and affluent middle class with disposable income to spend on home improvement. As this middle class grows, so too does the demand for high-quality and stylish home decor products, which is helping to drive the growth of the home decor industry in India.

Another important factor that influences the demand for home decor products in India is the increasing availability of affordable and high-quality products. As the home decor industry has grown, so too have the number of manufacturers and retailers, which has led to increased competition and lower prices for consumers. This has made home decor products more accessible to a wider range of consumers, and has helped to spur the growth of the home decor industry in India.

The supply chain for home decor products in India is complex and multi-layered, with a large number of manufacturers, wholesalers, and retailers involved. The majority of home decor products in India are manufactured domestically, although there is also a significant amount of imported goods, particularly from China. The distribution channels for home decor products in India are equally complex, with products being sold through a range of channels, including specialty stores, department stores, and online retailers.

The government plays an important role in regulating the home decor industry in India, including setting standards for product quality, establishing environmental regulations, and protecting consumers from fraud and scams. The government also provides support for the industry through programs designed to encourage entrepreneurship and innovation, and by providing incentives for manufacturers and retailers to invest in new technologies and production processes.

The home decor industry in India is a thriving and rapidly growing sector, driven by the growing middle class and increasing availability of affordable and high-quality products. The supply chain is complex, with a large number of players involved, and the government plays an important role in regulating the industry and supporting growth. As the Indian economy continues to grow and urbanization continues, it is likely that the demand for home decor products will continue to rise, and that the home decor industry in India will continue to grow and evolve.

"In Indian home decor, every element has a significance, every detail tells a story, making every space unique and special."

ꝏ

IX

The Impact of Indian Home Decor on Society

The home decor industry in India has had a profound impact on society, shaping the way that people live, work, and interact with their homes. In this chapter, we will examine the various ways in which home decor has impacted Indian society, including the creation of new jobs and economic opportunities, the influence of fashion and style, and the role of home decor in shaping cultural identity.

One of the most notable impacts of the home decor industry in India has been the creation of new jobs and economic opportunities. The growth of the home decor industry has led to an increase in the number of manufacturers, wholesalers, retailers, and service providers, providing employment opportunities for millions of people. The industry has also helped to spur economic growth and development in many regions, by creating demand for raw materials and supporting the growth of related industries, such as construction and transportation.

Another important impact of the home decor industry in India has been the influence of fashion and style. The home decor industry is constantly evolving and changing, reflecting the latest trends and styles in design, architecture, and interior decoration. This has had a significant impact on the way that people view their homes, and has helped to shape the way that homes are designed and decorated. The home decor industry has also been influenced by cultural trends, such as the rise of minimalist and eco-friendly design, which have helped to drive changes in the industry and in the way that people decorate their homes.

The impact of home decor on cultural identity is perhaps one of the most important and long-lasting effects of the industry. Home decor has the power to shape the way that people view themselves and their place in the world, by reflecting the cultural values, traditions, and beliefs of a society. In India, home decor has long been an expression of cultural identity, with regional styles and traditional design elements reflecting the diversity of the country. This has helped to create a rich and varied home decor landscape, and has contributed to the cultural richness and diversity of India.

The home decor industry in India has had a profound impact on society, creating new jobs and economic opportunities, shaping fashion and style, and influencing cultural identity. The industry continues to evolve and change, reflecting the latest trends and styles in design, architecture, and interior decoration. As the Indian economy continues to grow and urbanization continues, it is likely that the impact of home decor on society will continue to be felt, and that the industry will continue to play an important role in shaping the way that people live, work, and interact with their homes.

"Indian home decor is not just a visual delight, it is a sensory experience, evoking emotions and memories of a rich cultural legacy."

ꕥ

X

The Future of Indian Home Decor

The home decor industry in India has come a long way since its early beginnings, and the future of the industry looks bright, with many exciting trends and innovations on the horizon. In this chapter, we will explore the key drivers that are shaping the future of Indian home decor, and examine the various trends and developments that are likely to have a major impact on the industry in the years to come.

One of the key drivers of the future of Indian home decor is technology. Advances in digital technologies, such as 3D printing and virtual and augmented reality, are helping to revolutionize the way that people design and decorate their homes. For example, virtual reality and augmented reality can be used to create virtual mock-ups of a room, allowing people to see what their space will look like before making any physical changes. This is helping to make home decor more accessible and affordable, and is likely to have a major impact on the industry in the years to come.

Another important driver of the future of Indian home decor is sustainability. There is an increasing awareness of the environmental impact of home decor and a growing desire for environmentally friendly products and materials. This is leading to a rise in the use of recycled and eco-friendly materials, such as bamboo, cork, and recycled glass, and is helping to drive changes in the way that people design and decorate their homes. The trend towards sustainability is also likely to have a major impact on the home decor industry, as consumers become more conscious of their impact on the environment and seek out products and materials that are more environmentally friendly.

The growth of the middle class and the rise of urbanization are also likely to have a major impact on the future of Indian home decor. As people become more affluent and move into cities, they are looking for ways to create comfortable and stylish living spaces that reflect their individual tastes and lifestyles. This is leading to a rise in demand for high-end home decor products and services, and is driving the development of new and innovative home decor products and services.

Finally, the increasing diversity of Indian society is likely to have a major impact on the future of Indian home decor. As India continues to become more diverse, with people from different regions, cultures, and religions living and working together, there is an increasing desire to reflect this diversity in the design and decoration of homes. This is leading to a rise in the use of traditional and regional design elements, as well as the creation of new and innovative design styles that reflect the unique and diverse nature of Indian society.

The future of Indian home decor is shaped by many exciting trends and developments, including the rise of technology, the trend towards sustainability, the growth of the middle class and urbanization, and the increasing diversity of Indian society. These trends and developments are likely to have a major impact on the industry in the years to come, driving changes in the way that people design and decorate their homes and shaping the future of Indian home decor.

"From rustic and earthy to sleek and modern, the diversity of Indian home decor is a reflection of the diversity of our people."

ꕥ

XI

The Legacy of Indian Home Decor

India is a land of rich cultural heritage, which has been passed down through generations. The legacy of Indian home decor is an integral part of this rich cultural tapestry. It is the reflection of India's art, history, traditions, and customs. Over the centuries, Indian home decor has undergone many transformations and has been influenced by various styles, but the underlying elements of tradition and spirituality have remained intact.

The legacy of Indian home decor is embodied in the intricate designs and patterns that adorn the walls and ceilings of traditional homes. The use of vibrant colors and rich fabrics is also an essential aspect of Indian home decor. These elements reflect the diverse cultural influences that have shaped Indian home decor over the years. From the use of intricate carvings and embellishments in the Mughal era to the influence of British colonialism, Indian home decor has been influenced by a variety of styles and aesthetics.

Another important aspect of the legacy of Indian home decor is the use of natural materials, such as wood, stone, and clay. These materials are still widely used in modern Indian homes and are considered to be a symbol of simplicity and authenticity. The use of natural materials also reflects the strong connection that Indian culture has with nature and the environment.

In addition to the traditional elements, Indian home decor has also been influenced by modern design trends and technology. The use of modern materials and technologies has allowed for new and innovative ways of decorating homes. This has led to a new generation of Indian home decor designers who are pushing the boundaries of traditional design and incorporating new and creative elements into their work.

The legacy of Indian home decor is also embodied in the unique and intricate craftsmanship that is found in traditional Indian furniture and accessories. From the hand-carved wooden doors and windows to the intricate embroidery on cushions and curtains, the attention to detail and the passion for craftsmanship are evident in every aspect of traditional Indian home decor.

The legacy of Indian home decor is a rich and diverse tapestry of cultural influences, traditional elements, and modern innovations. It is a reflection of the rich cultural heritage of India and a testament to the creativity and passion of the Indian people. This legacy continues to inspire and influence the current generation of Indian home decor designers, and it will undoubtedly continue to shape the future of Indian home decor for generations to come.

"The legacy of Indian home decor will endure, as it continues to inspire and influence the world with its beauty and richness."

ꕥ

Modern Indian Home Interior

Other Books Of The Author

1. The Moments When I Met God
2. Kashiyile Theertha Pathangal
3. GURU GYAN VANI
4. Abhiprerak Gita
5. ASSI SE JAIN GHAT TAK
6. Hopelessness of Arjuna
7. The Soul and It's True Nature
8. Sense of Action (Karma)
9. Action through Wisdom
10. Action through Wisdom
11. THEORY AND PRACTICAL OF EVERY ACTION
12. LOGICAL UNDERSTANDING OF THE SUPREME
13. THE IMPERISHABLE SUPREME
14. Yatra Nishadraj se Hanuman Ghat Tak
15. Yatra Karnatak Ghat se Raja Ghat Tak
16. Yatra Pandey Ghat se Prayagraj Ghat Tak
17. Yatra Ranjendra Prasad Ghat se Dattatreya Ghat Tak
18. YaatraSindhiya Ghat se Gwaliar Ghat Tak
19. Yatra Mangala Gauri Ghat se Hanuman Gadhi Ghat Tak
20. Yatra Gaay Ghat Se Nishad Ghat Tak
21. MAA GANGA, GHATEN EVM UTSAV
22. Ganga Arti Dev Deepavali evam Any Utsav
23. Potentials of Digitalized India
24. VEDIC CONSCIOUSNESS
25. A Brief Introduction to Vedic Science
26. Kashi ke Barah Jyotirling
27. IMPACT OF MOTIVATION
28. Let's have a Milky Way Journey
29. Color Therapy in a Nutshell

30. Rigveda in a Nutshell
31. Yajurveda in a Nutshell
32. Samveda in a Nutshell
33. Atharva Veda in a Nutshell
34. Ayushman Bhava - Ayurveda
35. Srimad Bhagavad Gita and Upanishad Connection
36. Srimad Bhagavad Gita - an attempt to summarize each chapter.
37. Facts and Impact of Nakshatra
38. Astro Gems - NAVARATNA
39. Ekadashi - A Concise Overview
40. A Concise View of Hanuman Chalisa
41. Inspirational Gita
42. Nakshatraranyam
43. Summary of 18 Mahapuranas
44. Synopsis of 18 Upa Puranas
45. Rigvediya Upanishads
46. Shukla Yajurvediya Upanishads
47. Krishna Yajurvediya Upanishads
48. Samavediya Upanishads
49. Atharvavediya Upanishads
50. The Seven Great Sages
51. From Rocket Scientist to President Dr. APJ Abdul Kalam
52. The Visionary's Voice - Quotes of Dr. APJ Abdul Kalam
53. The Wisdom of Swami Vivekananda: Insights and Inspiration from a Legendary Spiritual Teacher
54. Ayurvedic Remedies from the Garden
55. Sages and Seers
56. Rising Strong – Motivational Stories of Women
57. Beyond Flames -Mystery stories of Funeral Ghat Manikarnika
58. The Origins of Tulsi: A Look at the Mythological Roots of the Plant"

59. The Holistic Cow: A Look at the Physical, Spiritual, and Cultural Importance of Cows in India
60. Arts of Healing
61. Exploring the Divine
62. Understanding Five Elements
63. The Etymology of Ram
64. Symbols of India
65. Voice of Change (About Speeches of Great Men)
66. She Speaks (About Speeches of Great Women)
67. Patriotism on Celluloid – Brief About Patriotic Films
68. The Music of Motivation: A Brief Guide to Inspirational Film Songs
69. **Unlocking the Secrets of the Dashopanishads**
70. A Cultural Mosaic
71. Ancient Traditions, Modern Minds
72. Ecos of Ancient Wisdom
73. Beneath the Surface
74. From Temples to Ashrams
75. Sages of the Subcontinent
76. The Art of Healling (Ayurveda, Yoga & Naturopathy)
77. Indian Kitchen
78. The Festivals of India
79. The Indian Epics Retold
80. The Power of Mantras
81. The Indian River Ganges
82. The Indian Architecture
83. Rites of Passage
84. The Indian Silk Road
85. The Indian Literature
86. The Indian Villages
87. The Indian Folks & Crafts
88. The Way of Buddha
89. The Ramayan of Tulsidas

90. Astrological Remedies
91. The Secret Power of Motivation
92. Secret of Developing your Inner Strength
93. The Secret Path to Motivation
94. The Art and Secret of Positive Thinking
95. The Secrets of Practicing Ethical Living
96. Indian Art and Painting
97. The Indian Herbalism
98. Bharatanatyam to Kathak
99. Exploring India's Astrological Remedies
100. The Indian Festival of Flowers
101. Indian Handicrafts
102. The Splashes of Joy – India's Colour Festival
103. The Indian Science of Astrology
104. The Indian Mythology
105. Path to Enlightenment
106. The Indian Spirituality for Children
107. Aromas of India
108. The Secrets of Healthy Relationships
109. Ancestral Ties
110. The Indian Street Food
111. Discovering America
112. The Indian Textile
113. Listening to Motivational Speeches
114. Taste of India
115. A Cultural Journey through Indian Nuptials
116. Motivational Quote for Change
117. Secret Strategies for Making Money
118. Secrets to Cultivate a Positive Mindset
119. A Tapestry of Cultures: Exploring India from Kashmir to Kanyakumari
120. Achieving Your Dreams with Resilience: Secret Strategies for Overcoming Obstacles

121. Innovative Startups - 25 Startup Ideas to Spark Your Business Creativity
122. Export Management: Strategies for Global Success
123. Exporting from India - A Step by Step Guide
124. Finance Fundamentals: Mastering Financial Management for Business Success
125. Global Growth Strategies for International Business Development
126. Marketing Mastery: Unlocking the Secrets of Modern Marketing
127. Operations Mastery: Managing the Flow of Value in Business
128. Strategic Business Management: Navigating the Modern Business Landscape
129. Human Resource Management Strategies for Building and Managing a High Performance Team
130. The Indian Landscapes and Nature: An Exploration Of India's Natural Beauty And Diversity
131. The Indian Street Performances: A Cultural Exploration of India's Street Performances
132. Affirming Your Self-Worth: Strategies for Achieving Emotional Wellbeing
133. Cultivating Self-Discipline: Secrets Methods for Achieving Your Goals
134. Embracing Change: Strategies for Adapting to Life's Challenges
135. Embracing Your Uniqueness: Secret Strategies for Living an Authentic Life
136. Finding Motivation in Despondency: Coping with Difficult Times
137. Embracing Change
138. Learning to Love Yourself
139. Managing Time for Yourself

140. Unlock the keys to Self-Motivation
141. Secret to Boost Confidence
142. Unlocking your Potential: A Path to Inner-strength & Success
143. Secrets to Develop Authentic Relationship
144. Secrets to Build a Successful Career
145. Secrets to Live with Gratitude
146. Secrets to Create a Life of Abundance
147. Secrets to Cultivate Self-Awareness
148. The Power of Helping Hands
149. Finding Your Passion
150. The Indian Mythical Creatures
151. The Indian Women Saints
152. The Wisdom of the Saints
153. "The Indian Royalty: A Cultural and Historical Exploration of India's Maharajas and their kingdom"
154. The Mystic Land: A Cultural and Spiritual Exploration of India"
155. India's Spiritual Legacy – Discovering the Cultural and Religious Significance of Bhakti Yoga.
156. The Indian Folktales: An Exploration of India's Oral Folklore Traditions
157. Steeping In History: A Look at India's Iconic Tea Culture
158. The Indian Way Of Life: An Exploration Of The Philosophy And Practices Of Indian Culture
159. From Silence to Sound: A Cultural and Historical Study of Indian Cinema
160. Chronicles of Indian Style: Tracing the Transformations of Traditional and Contemporary Fashion
161. Decorating India: A Journey Through the Traditions and Transformations of Home Design

CONTACT

DR. JAGADEESH PILLAI

MBA & PhD in Vedic Science

Four Times Guinness World Record Holder

Winner of Mahatma Gandhi Vishwa Shanti Puraskar and Global Peace Ambassador

Gemology, Astro & Vastu Consultant - Spiritual Counselor

Consultant for designing World Record Ideas

Efficient Tarot Card Reader

9839093003

myrichindia@gmail.com

drjagadeeshpillai@facebook

drjagadeeshpillai@instagram
jagadeeshpillai@youtube

www. JAGADEESHPILLAI.com

|| LOKAHA SAMASTHAHA SUKHINO BHAVANTU ||

9 798889 597377

Printed by Libri Plureos GmbH in Hamburg,
Germany